LESSONS FROM THE SHEPHERD

30 Days in Psalm 23

Jared Dyson

Dedication

To the Good Shepherd,
and to all who are learning to trust His leading.

Introduction

Psalm 23 is one of the most familiar passages in all of Scripture. Many of us have heard it read at moments of comfort, loss, and reflection. Its words are familiar, yet its depth is often unexplored. This Psalm invites us not to rush, but to slow down and consider what it truly means to live under the care of the Shepherd.

David's words were not written from a place of ease or perfection. They flowed from a life that had experienced both green pastures and deep valleys. As a former shepherd himself, David understood the responsibilities of caring for sheep, and he used that understanding to reflect on his relationship with God. Through this Psalm, we are invited into that same reflection—to see God not only as powerful and eternal, but as present, personal, and faithful.

Lessons from the Shepherd is designed as a 30-day journey through Psalm 23. Each day focuses on a phrase or theme from the Psalm, offering reflection, life application, prayer, and journaling prompts. This devotional is not meant to be rushed or completed perfectly. Instead, it is an invitation to sit with Scripture, listen for God's voice, and allow space for honest reflection.

You may choose to complete one day at a time or linger longer on a particular reflection. Some days may feel deeply personal, while others may quietly encourage your heart. Wherever you find yourself, know that there is no pressure to perform—only an invitation to walk closely with the Shepherd.

My prayer is that as you move through these pages, you will be reminded that you are known, cared for, and never walking alone. May this time of reflection lead you to greater trust, deeper peace, and a renewed awareness of the goodness and mercy that follow you all the days of your life.

TABLE OF CONTENTS

DAY 15

DAY 16

DAY 17

DAY 18

DAY 19

DAY 20

DAY 21

DAY 22

DAY 23

DAY 24

DAY 25

DAY 26

DAY 27

DAY 28

DAY 29

DAY 30

DAY 1

The LORD

Psalm 23:1 (KJV)
"The LORD is my shepherd; I shall not want."

Reflection

It is no secret how David felt about God as he begins Psalm 23. He begins by focusing on the word the LORD. This is the name Jehovah, meaning the existing or eternal one. This was a moment of reflection for David on exactly who God was.

God was not a mythical character that David had heard about. David had certainly heard the stories of those who had experienced God in days past, but this was David's moment of personal reflection. David was reflecting on the fact that the LORD was the one who had created everything. He was the one who was in control of everything. From the foundations of the world, Jehovah had existed.

But it was more than just God's prior existence. It was a current experience in David's life. David did not just stop with the comment about the LORD. He continued by saying the LORD is. He was not just God in the past, but this was God being present. David was fully reflecting on who the LORD Jehovah was.

Life Application

We may not always recall every moment we experienced the LORD in our lives. Yet, just like David, we can reflect on many moments in our lives when we have experienced the LORD in unique ways. One of the most impactful experiences would be the moment that we accept Christ as Savior. Once we have experienced the life change that Jesus can bring, it is a moment we will remember.

Beyond that life-changing moment, we have all experienced God in other areas of our lives. Maybe it was the first moment he ever spoke to our hearts. It could be the first time he intervened in a situation in our lives. The God who intervened in your life in those moments is the same God who laid out the foundations of the world. The same Jehovah whom David is referring to here.

He is not just a story from the past. The LORD is ever present and real in our lives today. Today, focus on seeing God not for what he has done, but for who he is!

Prayer

Lord, you are the eternal one. The one who existed before all things and who is present with me now. Many times, I may only think of the things you have done for me, rather than who you truly are. Today, help me to remember that you are not a distant and forgotten God, but one who is here with me now. Help me to see the moments in my life where you have revealed yourself in a fresh way. Teach me to walk in awareness of you as a God who is active and alive in my life today. Amen.

Personal Reflection

• What is the first moment that you remember experiencing the LORD in your life?
• In what ways has God intervened in your life since that first moment?

• How do you typically think about God – do you think more about what he has done for you or for who he is?

• What do the words "The LORD is" mean to you at this point in time of your life?

Quiet Consideration

Slow your pace and sit with the truth that the LORD is not distant or abstract, but present and personal.

Consider what it means for Him to be *your* Shepherd in this season of life.

As you reflect quietly, allow yourself to rest in the assurance that your life is not sustained by your strength alone, but by the care of the One who knows you completely.

DAY 2

My Shepherd

Psalm 23:1 (KJV)
"The LORD is my shepherd; I shall not want."

Reflection

After David's moment of reflection on who God is, he identifies God as "my shepherd." This is a direct statement about how God is the one who tends his flock. This is not just someone who simply takes care of some animals by dropping off some food and filling a water bucket. This is someone who is intimately involved in the care of the sheep.

The Shepherd is the one who does everything for the sheep. He provides food and water, protection, guidance, and so much more. The shepherd knows his flock. He knows their strengths and weaknesses. He understands their temptations and struggles. He guides them through their path but will also carry them when they become too weak to continue on.

David recognizes the responsibilities of the shepherd because he himself was a shepherd. He knew what it was like to risk his own life for the sheep. His firsthand experience made this a personal connection with God. David knew the importance of having a shepherd for the sheep, and he realized that he was dependent on God as his shepherd.

Life Application

Few of us may have firsthand experience as a shepherd like David. Yet, we have all had the experience of God as our shepherd! We have experienced the provision of God on many occasions in our lives. We have experienced his protection, his love, his compassion, and so much more. But for David, this went beyond the experience to the point of understanding his dependence.

The sheep do not always realize that they are dependent upon the shepherd. In fact, sheep will often wander from the fold because they become distracted in their own thoughts and ways. If you are like me, that sounds very familiar. I often become distracted by things in this world and the ideas that I may know what is best. It causes me to lose sight of my dependence on the shepherd.

Each of us possesses free will and the choice to follow or not to follow God. So often we become distracted and lose sight of the fact that we are fully dependent on him. He is our shepherd, and we are his sheep. In every circumstance and situation, God is the one who provides for and cares for us. He is more than just the LORD who is ever present. He is our shepherd, the one who we are fully dependent upon for everything in our lives.

Prayer

Lord, you are the shepherd of my soul. You have cared for me fully, wonderfully, and faithfully. There are many times in my life when I may forget that I am dependent upon you. I often become distracted by my own thoughts, rely on my own understanding, and wander in directions that may lead me astray from you. Thank you for protecting me from danger when I am unaware and bringing me back into the flock when I wander astray. Help me to have an awareness that my life was never designed to walk alone, but with a shepherd guiding me each step of the way. Amen.

Journal Reflection

• In what ways have you experienced God's care as your shepherd?

• Where do you see yourself becoming distracted from walking with the shepherd?

• How would your daily life choices change if you were to follow the shepherd as you should?

Quiet Consideration

Slow your pace and sit with the truth that the LORD is not distant or abstract, but present and personal.

Consider what it means for Him to be *your* Shepherd in this season of life.

As you reflect quietly, allow yourself to rest in the assurance that your life is not sustained by your strength alone, but by the care of the One who knows you completely.

DAY 3

It is not all about you

Psalm 23:1 (KJV)
"The LORD is my shepherd; I shall not want."

Reflection

As David recognizes his dependence on the shepherd, he recognizes something. Life is often viewed through the personal lens. We often only think of things that impact or affect us, forgetting that life is not all about us. David could no doubt reflect on the moments when he was a shepherd and remember that there were more sheep in the fold than just one. In fact, he no doubt had countless sheep that he was caring for and had to care for each of them as if they were the only one.

As David continues, I am drawn to the next word in the verse, "I." David was not focused on the other sheep around him. He was only focused on himself at this point in time. Some may argue that this was a point of personal reflection for David, and that is true. In those moments of reflection, we are all often consumed in our own self-thought.

In just this one word, however, we are reminded of this. We are reminded that we can often become so consumed with thoughts of ourselves and our own personal situation, that we might overlook the circumstances that there are other sheep around us in need of the shepherd's care too!

Life Application

As we continue reflecting on Psalm 23, how often do we think of others as we go through our lives? We know that millions of people exist around us each and every day. Many of them face similar challenges and circumstances as we all do. We all have one thing in common: we all need the shepherd!

Many people go through this life believing that they are able to exist on their own apart from God. The truth is no one is capable of existing without a shepherd. They may not be aware of the need for a shepherd in their life, but they need a shepherd. Many never recognize that they have experienced the mercy and grace of God in their lives. They believe in accidents and luck.

As we consider our relationship with the shepherd, do our lives point others to Christ so that they might see how they genuinely need a shepherd? Do we give credit to God for all that he does so that others might see him? Many will never see God as the shepherd in the Bible, but they may see him as the shepherd of your life in how you interact with him each day.

Prayer

Lord, thank you for all that you do in caring for me and meeting me where I am. It is often easy for me to see life through my own needs, struggles, and circumstances. I can often become focused on myself to the point that I forget that there is a large flock. You care for each as if they were the only one. Help me to see beyond myself. Open my eyes to those around me who may be wandering, weary, or unaware of their need for a shepherd. Help me to live my life in a way that points others to the Shepherd of mercy and grace. Let my life be a testimony to others for all that you have done, and draw others close to you. Amen.

Personal Reflection

• How do you tend to view life through your own personal experiences and needs?

• Who are the "other sheep" that God has placed in your life right now?

• What is one way you can intentionally reflect the shepherd's care to someone else this week?

Quiet Consideration

Slow your pace and sit with the truth that the LORD is not distant or abstract, but present and personal.

Consider what it means for Him to be *your* Shepherd in this season of life.

As you reflect quietly, allow yourself to rest in the assurance that your life is not sustained by your strength alone, but by the care of the One who knows you completely.

DAY 4

All our needs

Psalm 23:1 (KJV)
"The LORD is my shepherd; I shall not want."

Reflection

David recognized that life was filled with needs. He needed provision, protection, comfort, guidance, and so much more. As we have already described, David recognized his dependence on the shepherd because of his experience as a shepherd. He knew the immense responsibility of the shepherd to meet the needs of the sheep. The sheep often did not realize that they had these needs!

David was not saying that there was nothing in life to be desired. David could no doubt look into the homes of those around him and see things that he wanted. David was a human just like us. Maybe his neighbor had a new chariot, and David thought it was amazing. Or perhaps his neighbor chose a new paint color, or was outside working with a new gadget, and David could have felt the need to have one. There was no doubt many things that David could have desired.

What David is saying here is that of all the things he needed in life, the shepherd had met each one. As David examined his life, there was nothing critical that was missing. The shepherd had carefully and diligently met each and every need.

Life Application

It is very easy for us to become confused about the difference between wants and needs. We can see the new cars, new homes, new tech gadgets, and we can often say something like, "I need one of those!" But those are not truly classified as needs.

The shepherd knows the things in life that we truly need. He knows when we need comfort, protection, guidance, and provision. Before we even know what we have need of, he already knows the need and how he can meet that need.

That is not to say we will go through life without wants. Our human nature lends itself to desire. Scripture gives clear warnings about those desires. We are told not to desire the things of our neighbor but rather hunger and thirst after the things of God! Why? Because God knows exactly what we need and how to meet those needs.

Our desire should not be set on the things of this world, but the things of God. We should hunger and thirst after God's purpose and will for our lives. He knows exactly what we need. We should trust the shepherd to provide.

Prayer

Lord, you know me completely. You understand my needs even when I confuse them with wants. Things around me can often distract, causing me to believe that they will somehow satisfy my heart. You remind me that you are the one who truly provides what matters. Thank you for meeting my needs each day, even when I may not recognize it. Help me to trust in you when my desires pull my attention elsewhere. Teach me to hunger and thirst for your will and purpose above all else. Align my heart with you so that I desire you more than anything this world can offer. Amen.

Personal Reflection

• What are some things in life that you currently view as "needs" that may actually be wants?

• Look back over your life. Where can you see moments that God has faithfully met your needs?

• How do desires and wants impact your ability to focus on God's purpose and plan for your life?

Quiet Consideration

Slow your pace and sit with the truth that the LORD is not distant or abstract, but present and personal.

Consider what it means for Him to be *your* Shepherd in this season of life.

As you reflect quietly, allow yourself to rest in the assurance that your life is not sustained by your strength alone, but by the care of the One who knows you completely.

DAY 5

The Shepherd's force

Psalm 23:2 (KJV)
"He maketh me to lie down in green pastures: he leadeth me beside the still waters."

Reflection

As David continues to write here in Psalm 23, I can imagine he is reflecting on his time as a shepherd again. He writes the first few words here that are translated in the KJV as "He maketh me." In these words, it is a statement that, at times, being a shepherd requires the use of force to compel the sheep.

This force can come about for many reasons. Many focus on the latter words of this verse, which talk about being forced to rest. That is certainly a possibility. A shepherd will also use force at various times for other things. For example, a shepherd might use force to guide the sheep back into the fold as they wander astray. In this moment, they might reach out with their shepherd's hook and pull the sheep back closer, preventing them from walking into danger. This might go against what the sheep wanted on their own, but it is what was best for the sheep.

The force of the shepherd may be stronger in some moments compared to others. For example, a gentle nudge may be all it takes to encourage one sheep from wandering astray. For another, it may be a more forceful pulling away from impending danger. The shepherd knows the exact force required to get the sheep to listen.

Life Application

Just like the sheep, we can often require the shepherd's force to cause us to come back into the fold. God knows exactly what force it takes to compel us to go where he wants us to go. Maybe it is just a gentle nudge to remind us that we need to stay close to the shepherd. At other times, it may be more forceful. The real challenge for us is how quickly we will listen.

The force of the shepherd often changes as we ignore those moments of gentle nudging. Perhaps he speaks to us in that still small voice, reminding us that danger is near. Yet, we ignore that voice and continue on. The next time, the voice may not be so small. It may become more forceful and powerful.

At some point, the shepherd moves beyond simple words and into action. Have you found yourself in that moment with God where he moved beyond gentle reminders and into a more forceful action, preventing you from danger and harm? It's a reminder of how much the shepherd loves us, but the importance of listening to the shepherd when he speaks!

Prayer

Lord, thank you for caring enough for me to intervene in my life when I wander from you. I may not always listen when you speak gently. I may often act just like a sheep, being distracted, stubborn, or convinced that I know what is best. You see the dangers and paths before me that I do not see. Help me to recognize your voice quickly and respond in humility and trust. Remind me that you do not guide me out of punishment, but from love. Teach me to listen before force is required and shape my heart to follow you willingly. Help me trust that your way is always best. Amen.

Personal Reflection

• Can you recall a moment when God nudged you away from something that was not good for you?

• What are some areas in your life where you might be ignoring God's gentle guidance right now?

• What would life look like if you were to respond more quickly to the Shepherd's leading?

Quiet Consideration

Slow your pace and sit with the truth that the LORD is not distant or abstract, but present and personal.

Consider what it means for Him to be *your* Shepherd in this season of life.

As you reflect quietly, allow yourself to rest in the assurance that your life is not sustained by your strength alone, but by the care of the One who knows you completely.

DAY 6

Finding true rest

Psalm 23:2 (KJV)
"He maketh me to lie down in green pastures: he leadeth me beside the still waters."

Reflection

David continues to think about the LORD as his shepherd and compares it to the times in his life when he was a shepherd. He recalls being forceful with his sheep, and at times, that meant forcing them into green pastures where they would lie down and rest.

The original text uses a word for rest here that means fully stretched out. This was not a moment of gentle rest where the sheep might quickly jump up and continue moving. This was a moment where the sheep were fully stretched out, fully resting in the protection of their shepherd. The shepherd did not lead the sheep to this place of rest where danger could overtake them. This was a place of true rest and comfort, where the shepherd could watch over the sheep.

At times, the sheep would not lie down out of worry or distress. They can be easily scared of the slightest noise. But the shepherd may use the nudging force to make them lie down. The sheep take comfort in the shepherd at this moment. He has removed their fears, allowing them to fully stretch out and rest.

Life Application

We are often scared and nervous about the slightest things in life. Let one piece of bad news or potential danger come into our minds, and we can be overcome with worry and anxiety. It can cause us to enter into a place where we cannot rest! That's where the shepherd comes in!

Just like the shepherd David describes, God can calm all of our fears and remove all of our distress. Life brings about so many things we can worry about. Health conditions, financial challenges, job concerns, and so much more. If we focus on these things, we can find ourselves missing the full rest and relaxation that the shepherd wants us to have!

For us to find true rest, we must fully trust in the shepherd. Think back to that moment of the sheep fully stretching out and resting. That is a full trust and reliance in the shepherd that, no matter what may come into their lives, they know the shepherd will protect them. It takes this type of full faith and trust to find true rest.

Just like the sheep, we know that our Shepherd is more than capable of taking care of all the worries and fears that may prevent us from finding true rest. The challenge is that we often do not fully trust. We try to hold on to things on our own, rather than giving them entirely to God.

Prayer

Lord, it can be easy for my heart to become restless and afraid. I often carry worries that I should trust to you. Even when you lead me to a place of rest, I can often act just like a sheep, remaining alert, guarded, and ready to jump at the first sign of trouble. Thank you for always watching over me and help me to trust in you completely. Remove the fears from my life and help me find comfort in knowing that you are nearby and protecting me. Teach me to let go of my worries and anxiety in life. Help me to know that my life is secure in your hands. Amen.

Personal Reflection

• What worries or fears keep you from fully resting in God's care?

• When anxiety or uncertainty enters your mind, how do you normally respond?

• Has God proven himself to you in times of fear or distress? What keeps you from fully trusting him in those moments?

Quiet Consideration

Pause here and allow your heart to grow still.

Reflect on the ways you may be resisting rest or striving to lead yourself instead of being led.

In this quiet moment, consider what it would look like to trust the Shepherd enough to slow down and follow where He is guiding, even when the path is unfamiliar.

DAY 7

Comforts of home

Psalm 23:2 (KJV)
"He maketh me to lie down in green pastures: he leadeth me beside the still waters."

Reflection

It is hard to think of a green pasture as somewhere to call home. That is exactly what the sheep do, however. The shepherd finds a place of green pasture, and the sheep lie down and call that place home. If you study the original text, that is what you find the original word to be. It means abode, or a home.

In the time of David, those green pastures would often be temporary homes. They would venture from area to area, searching for a place to have their flock settle for a short time. The shepherd would look to feed the sheep, enabling them to be fully satisfied, and then provide a place for them to settle down.

For the sheep, the area was not a place of abode without the shepherd. They were fully dependent on the shepherd for everything. Unless the shepherd was near, it wasn't home. It wasn't a place of comfort or rest. But in this instance, the shepherd was near, and the flock was led to a green pasture where they could lie down comfortably and enjoy the comforts of home.

Life Application

There are many aspects of life today that prevent the home from being a place of comfort for many people. For some, home is a place of turmoil and heartbreak. It could be from being part of a broken home, a neglectful home, a violent home, or many other things that may cause a home not to have comfort. Finding comfort in a home starts in one place, with the shepherd!

We may find ourselves having a home in this life, where we can try to escape the troubles of this world. But that home will never have the real comfort it could have apart from God. Our homes must be built on a foundation of faith and trust in the Shepherd.

I am reminded of the words of Joshua 24:15. Each of us faces the decision of choosing who we will serve. You can place the things of this world first, trusting and hoping in something that will let you down. In those, you will find that your home lacks many things.

Instead, we should resolve as Joshua did, saying, "As for me and my house, we will serve the LORD." Our homes should be a place of dependence and comfort in the Shepherd. When the Shepherd is first in your home, it is only at that moment that you can enjoy the true comforts of home.

Prayer

Lord, thank you for leading me to the green pastures of life and a place to call home. While our home in this world is temporary, you can make it a place of comfort. There are many times my ideas of a home are shaped by past hurt, brokenness, or disappointment as opposed to your presence. You remind me that true comfort is not found in a place, but in being near you. I invite you to come into my home. Bring peace, bring healing, and bring comfort where it is needed. Help me build my home on trust and faith in you. May your presence be foundational to my home. Amen.

Personal Reflection

• What comes to your mind when you think of home?

• How have you tried to find security and comfort apart from God's presence?

• Is your home a place where the Shepherd is welcomed?

• Can you honestly say, "As for me and my house, we will serve the LORD?"

Quiet Consideration

Pause here and allow your heart to grow still.

Reflect on the ways you may be resisting rest or striving to lead yourself instead of being led.

In this quiet moment, consider what it would look like to trust the Shepherd enough to slow down and follow where He is guiding, even when the path is unfamiliar.

DAY 8

The Shepherd's guidance

Psalm 23:2 (KJV)
"He maketh me to lie down in green pastures: he leadeth me beside the still waters."

Reflection

David has already examined the role of the shepherd in many different ways, as we examined the first two verses of this Psalm. As we enter the next phrase of verse two, he begins by speaking about the guidance of the shepherd.

This is not the correction of the shepherd, as we looked at before. Rather than the sheep venturing out on their own, in this moment, they are actively following the shepherd. The shepherd is leading them toward something, and the sheep are not focused on where they are going or anything around them. They are focused on following the shepherd.

One might quickly argue that life as a shepherd becomes more enjoyable when the sheep are following as they should. The truth is, whether the sheep follow the shepherd or the shepherd forcefully guides them, it does not change the shepherd's responsibility. He is still fully responsible for the well-being of the sheep. When the sheep follow the shepherd as is described here, it does have a benefit for the sheep. It is in those moments that the sheep will find themselves closer to the shepherd and building a stronger relationship with the shepherd.

Life Application

Closeness to the shepherd is something that cannot be replaced. It is in those moments that the sheep can easily hear the shepherd's voice. At times, they may even brush up against the shepherd's leg as they walk. How amazing a thought if our relationship to God could be so close!

22

We often try to follow God from a distance. We may try to hide our faith from those we work with, our neighbors, and even our close friends. We want to have faith in God, but we do not want others to judge us for having faith or living a life dedicated fully to God. Instead of walking close to God, we find ourselves at a distance, where we can easily be distracted and wander away.

Our hearts should be set on following closely to the Shepherd. We should want to live our lives in a way that we can hear his voice easily. We should want to feel his presence walking beside us each day as we go through our lives. This is not accomplished by following the Shepherd from a distance. It is only found by following him closely and living a life that is dedicated to him. Our focus should be on following the shepherd, no matter who may see us or what they may think about how closely we are following him.

Prayer

Lord, you have invited me to a closer walk with you. I confess that there are times that may follow from a distance. I find myself close enough to know you are there, but far enough to feel safe from the opinions of those around me. This allows fear, distraction, and self-consciousness to keep space between us. Help me to hear your voice clearly and your presence beside me every step of my life. Help me to set my heart on following you fully, without any hesitation or reservation. Closeness to you is always worth the cost. Give me the courage to follow you openly, inviting others to see me walking with you every day. Draw me near and help me remain where your presence is most clearly felt. Amen.

Personal Reflection

• In what areas of your life do you find yourself following God from a distance?

• How do you sense the change in your ability to hear God's voice when you are close to him versus when you are distant?

• Is there a situation where you have been hesitant to be open about your faith?

Quiet Consideration

Pause here and allow your heart to grow still.

Reflect on the ways you may be resisting rest or striving to lead yourself instead of being led.

In this quiet moment, consider what it would look like to trust the Shepherd enough to slow down and follow where He is guiding, even when the path is unfamiliar.

DAY 9

Refreshing still waters

Psalm 23:2 (KJV)
"He maketh me to lie down in green pastures: he leadeth me beside the still waters."

Reflection

As David continues to describe the shepherd's guidance, he comes to a description of the shepherd leading the sheep to the still waters. These waters represent nourishment and refreshment for the sheep. This is not a running stream of water, like a river. Instead, it's a description of a still water that may be running in a small, but shallow channel.

If the shepherd were to lead the sheep to extremely deep waters, the sheep would be in danger of drowning. If the water was rushing violently, the sheep would be in danger of being washed away. Those noises could also scare the sheep, placing them in more danger. The image described by David is also not one of being a mud-ridden area, either. If this were the case, the sheep would be at risk of being mired in the mud and unable to move.

Instead, the shepherd has chosen to guide the sheep into a place of still water. One where they can comfortably find refreshment and nourishment without all of the potential fears and troubles that could come upon them. This is a needed refreshment for sustenance and in moments of exhaustion. The shepherd knows precisely what is needed!

Life Application

Perhaps you have already noticed that when we look to the world for comfort and nourishment, we have to be on guard constantly. The world might say that there are places of nourishment and comfort, but danger is all around! The waters might be deeper and more dangerous than they

25

appeared. Perhaps the current is stronger than you realized, and you are at risk of being swept away. Whenever the world is offering something, it always looks better on the surface, as the danger is hidden.

When we trust the shepherd to guide us to those places of nourishment, we can be confident that there is safety and security to be found. We do not have to worry about being swept away, pulled under, or mired in the mud. Instead, we can rest assured that we will be able to stand firm, receive the nourishment we need, and continue on following the shepherd.

Perhaps you find yourself at a crossroads in life, needing nourishment. Will you try to find it in the things of this world, or will you follow the Shepherd to a place of nourishment for your soul? While it may not seem too dangerous on the surface to find it in the world, the dangers are hidden. Rather than being nourished in the safety of the Shepherd, you may find yourself needing the Shepherd to come to your rescue.

Prayer

Lord, you know the place for my soul to find true refreshment. I may often be drawn to things that look appealing on the surface, failing to recognize the dangers that are present. In those places, I find that the nourishment leaves me weary and empty. Thank you for leading me with my best interest in mind. You guide me into stillness where my soul can be restored. Help me to trust your guidance and teach me to follow you even when the world offers appealing alternatives. Amen.

Personal Reflection

• Where do you look for refreshment when you feel tired or overwhelmed?

• Can you identify a time when something looked nourishing, but ended up being unsafe or unhelpful?

• What step is God inviting you to take in following him toward healthier, safer nourishment for your soul?

Quiet Consideration

Pause here and allow your heart to grow still.

Reflect on the ways you may be resisting rest or striving to lead yourself instead of being led.

In this quiet moment, consider what it would look like to trust the Shepherd enough to slow down and follow where He is guiding, even when the path is unfamiliar.

DAY 10

The ultimate restoration

Psalm 23:3 (KJV)
"He restoreth my soul: he leadeth me in the paths of righteousness for his name's sake."

Reflection

David concludes his description of how the shepherd guides the sheep to a place of nourishment by proceeding into the next verse and speaking of restoration. The word restoreth here in the original text means to bring back, to return to, or to return life to. It is the idea that what was slowly failing to live has been fully restored and given renewed purpose.

The walks with the shepherd in David's day could be painfully long. The sheep would find themselves weary. This is, again, not a reference to sheep that have gone astray and needing to be restored to the shepherd's care again. Instead, these were the sheep that were faithfully following the shepherd.

Just because the sheep were walking with and following the shepherd closely did not exclude them from becoming weary. It did not prevent them from being worn down by the walking and the journey. These sheep found themselves in need of restoration, even when they were right beside the shepherd the entire time.

Life Application

I love to look at antique cars that have been restored. There is just something amazing about taking something that looks worn out and useless and providing it with a purpose once again. Once, I saw one called "the ultimate restoration." While the restoration was impressive, it was far from the ultimate restoration in my mind.

The ultimate restoration belongs to God. He is the one who can take something like me, as worn out and useless as I can appear to many people, and give me a renewed purpose in life once again. Maybe you find yourself in that type of season in your life. Perhaps the circumstances and challenges of life have caused you to become weary and worn. Maybe you find yourself in a place needing restoration.

God, as our Shepherd, specializes in restoration. He can take what is weary and worn and give it new life and new purpose. Just because you find yourself worn from the journey in this life, does not mean that you are without a purpose for God!

God can guide you to a place of ultimate restoration. When you feel as though your life has been ripped away and torn apart, he can make you whole again. No matter what you may be facing, God is the one who can give you the restoration that you need!

Prayer

Lord, thank you for seeing me in my weariness and loving me just as I am. There are moments when I feel worn down by life's journey. My body, mind, and spirit may let me down even though my heart wants to follow you. At times, it feels as though I have no strength left. You have reminded me that weariness does not mean failure, and exhaustion does not remove purpose from my life. You are the one who restores life, renews hope, and brings beauty from what feels broken and worn. Help me trust you with my heart, mind, and soul to find true restoration. You are not finished with me yet. Give me a renewed purpose to continue to walk with you. Amen.

Personal Reflection

• How are you currently feeling weary or worn down?

• Have you ever felt like a failure due to being weary and worn?

• How have you experienced God's restoration in the past?

• What area in your life needs God's restoring touch today?

Quiet Consideration

Sit quietly and reflect on where your strength has been renewed or where it feels depleted.

Consider how the Shepherd restores not only your energy, but your direction and purpose.

As you remain still, allow this moment to remind you that restoration often comes as you continue walking faithfully with Him.

DAY 11

Following God's path

Psalm 23:3 (KJV)
"He restoreth my soul: he leadeth me in the paths of righteousness for his name's sake."

Reflection

After finding restoration in the shepherd, David returns to the idea of the shepherd leading the sheep once again. Now, the shepherd is leading the sheep in paths of righteousness. You could easily summarize this and say that David is saying that God is leading the sheep down God's path. He was leading the sheep to follow his will.

As the sheep are following the shepherd closely, they are not wandering into their own paths. Those paths lead to distractions and trouble. Instead, they are following the paths that were laid out in front of them. In this instance, it is God's path. The path that God has designated for the sheep to follow.

David said he was not following in his own will at this moment but instead trusting in God's will. David was not serving his own purpose but serving God's purpose. He was not following his plan for life but following God's plan for life. David was no longer living life for himself, but he was fully dedicated to living his life for God.

Life Application

Our human nature is to follow our plan for every aspect of our lives. We are told this from a young age. We are told to find something that we enjoy in life and to chase it. For some, those things are sports. For others, it's specific careers or educational pursuits. But are those paths the ones that God would have us follow?

31

God has a specific purpose and plan for each life. He knows the desires of our hearts and the things that bring us fulfillment. In each of those instances, his will for our lives is perfectly designed to bring us fulfillment as we follow his path and plan for our lives.

When we follow God's plan, we are no longer living our lives for ourselves. Our purpose is replaced with God's purpose. Our life plans become God's plans for our lives. Instead of choosing our own way, we follow God's will.

This requires more than just following God's guidance. It requires full submission to him. It means letting go of our own desires and ideas and fully embracing God's purpose and plan for our lives. This is an everyday, every moment sacrifice of ourselves and submission to the will of God.

Prayer

Lord, thank you for restoring my soul and leading me gently forward. I may often prefer my own plans, my own timing, and my own understanding of what my life should be. Surrender is not always easy, even when I trust you and want to follow you. Today, I want to place my life back in your hands. Lead me in your paths so that I might follow your will, not my will. Help me trust in your purpose over my own. Teach me to submit not out of obligation, but out of love and confidence that your way is the best. Help me to surrender my choices, desires, and direction to your will and to follow you faithfully. Amen.

Personal Reflection

• Where do you naturally default to your own plans rather than God's?

• How do you discern whether you are following God's path or your path?

• Is there an area of your life in which God is calling you into greater submission today?

Quiet Consideration

Sit quietly and reflect on where your strength has been renewed or where it feels depleted.

Consider how the Shepherd restores not only your energy, but your direction and purpose.

As you remain still, allow this moment to remind you that restoration often comes as you continue walking faithfully with Him.

DAY 12

The importance of righteousness

Psalm 23:3 (KJV)
"He restoreth my soul: he leadeth me in the paths of righteousness for his name's sake."

Reflection

David recognized that God was guiding him in a specific path through life. This path was not one of David's own design. Instead, it was one of God's design and purpose. As David reflected on the path that God was leading him on, one word came to mind: righteousness.

In the original meaning, the definition of the word translated righteousness here meant a path of morality, legality, and victory. It also carried the idea of being justified. If you think of morality, David was far from the perfect description of morality. He was a sinner, just like we are. Yet, David is acknowledging that when someone is following the path of God, it leads them to live a life of morality.

This does not mean a life of perfection. This is where the concept of victory comes in. This victory is through the justification we have in God. The path that God leads us on is one that will guide us to live morally, ethically, legally, but also recognizing that our lives are far from perfect. We are unable to live in this moral and ethical path on our own; it takes the Shepherd!

Life Application

We have all failed to live the lives God would have us live on our own. Our human nature is one of sin. While growing up, our parents and those around us may encourage us to live morally and ethically, that is not what comes naturally. Sin and following in our own path away from righteousness is what comes naturally.

David recognized that he was not able to live his life for God without victory over these things through the justification that the Shepherd brings. That justification is not found in anything that we accomplish on our own. Instead, it is found through the forgiveness of our sins.

If it were up to each of us to live a life of righteousness, we would always fall short and fail. The only way for us to live a life of righteousness is by finding forgiveness of our sins and completely giving our lives to Christ. If we do this, he will guide our lives to be morally and ethically responsible, leading us to victory over the things that would ultimately cause us to fail to meet the goal of righteousness.

Prayer

Lord, thank you for leading me on a path that I could never walk on my own. If left to myself, I would fall short of the righteousness that you desire from my life. My efforts are not enough on their own. You do not ask me to be perfect; you invite me to be forgiven and live a life that is justified and led by you. Thank you for the victory that comes through your grace. Help me to trust in you rather than striving to prove myself worthy. Guide my steps so that my life reflects your righteousness, shaped by forgiveness and dependence on you. Teach me to walk daily in your guidance and trust you to work in my life. Amen.

Personal Reflection

• Where do you feel the tension in life between wanting to live rightly and recognizing your limitations?

• How do you respond when you fall short of what God wants?

• In what areas of your life do you need to more fully rely on the Shepherd's guidance rather than your own effort?

Quiet Consideration

Sit quietly and reflect on where your strength has been renewed or where it feels depleted.

Consider how the Shepherd restores not only your energy, but your direction and purpose.

As you remain still, allow this moment to remind you that restoration often comes as you continue walking faithfully with Him.

DAY 13

Brand Ambassador

Psalm 23:3 (KJV)
"He restoreth my soul: he leadeth me in the paths of righteousness for his name's sake."

Reflection

As David wraps up the third verse of Psalm 23, he makes a unique declaration. Of all the reasons that God could do the things that he does, David declares in this moment that he is doing them for his name's sake. In other words, he is doing them so that his name might receive recognition and honor.

This was no doubt a different circumstance for David than many others. David was not used to doing things for recognition. The life of a shepherd was not one of significant recognition. It was one of immense sacrifice.

Which brings us to the question that David must have pondered here. Why would the LORD that we learned about in verse one want anything to do with us? Why would he take time away from everything else he has going on, to lead us to rest, guide us in his paths, and to offer a path of forgiveness from our sins? He did it all so that it might bring recognition to his name. He did it all so that he might be honored and glorified in all that was done.

Life Application

One of the new concepts in our society today is that of a brand ambassador. These are individuals who represent companies, or brands, on various media platforms. You might see them on social media videos and posts, in television ads, and more. They are the face of the item or brand they represent.

This is exactly what God has in mind for our lives. He has been our Shepherd so that his name might be honored. For that to happen, you and I are brand ambassadors for Christ. Our very salvation points back to the work that Christ did on the cross. His guidance, care, and direction in our lives point back to his love as our Shepherd.

Rather than basking in these things for ourselves, we should be pointing others back to the Shepherd! All of our words and actions should tell the world that we are not who we are on our own. We are who we are because of a loving Savior who gave his life for our sins and continues to provide for us as our Shepherd each day.

Prayer

Lord, thank you for caring for me in ways I never deserved. I am humbled to know that you lead, restore, forgive, and guide me, not for my own recognition, but for the honor of your name. You have shown me grace so that others might see who you are through my life. Help me to remember that everything you have done is meant to point back to you. Guard my heart from seeking attention, approval, or praise for myself. Instead, shape my words, actions, and attitudes so that they reflect you. Let my life faithfully honor your name, as a witness of your love. Let all that I do bring glory to you alone. Amen.

Personal Reflection

• How do you respond to God's blessings and care in your life? Do you bring attention to yourself or to God?

• In what ways does your life currently point others to the Shepherd?

• What does it mean to you to live your life "for his name's sake?"

• Is there an area of your life where God is inviting you to give him more glory?

Quiet Consideration

Sit quietly and reflect on where your strength has been renewed or where it feels depleted.

Consider how the Shepherd restores not only your energy, but your direction and purpose.

As you remain still, allow this moment to remind you that restoration often comes as you continue walking faithfully with Him.

DAY 14

Walking through the valley

Psalm 23:4 (KJV)
"Yea, though I walk through the valley of the shadow of death, I will fear no evil:"

Reflection

I can only imagine as David continues to pen the words to this Psalm as he reflects back on his time as a shepherd. He starts to think about how those paths of righteousness transitioned to valleys. Valleys were not uncommon in the geographical area around David. He was undoubtedly experienced in walking through areas where the hills rose up around him in the valley and cut off the light, leaving him in a state of darkness.

Valleys are a place of unknowns. On the hills surrounding the valley, it is unknown what dangers might be present. The shadows might prevent the ability to see clearly what lies ahead. David no doubt thought back to some of those valleys that he experienced as a shepherd. He probably remembers some of the dangers that he was exposed to.

As David thinks on these things, he also remembers his responsibility as the shepherd was to watch over the flock. No matter what danger might lie above the flock on the hill, or ahead of the flock in the valley, the shepherd was to lead the sheep and walk with them right through the middle of that valley. He never left the flock alone, always staying by their side.

Life Application

There are many times that we walk through the valleys of life spiritually. In those moments, it may feel like we are stuck in darkness all around us. There are times when we would love to just have a small bit of light so that we might see if there are dangers that lie ahead. Or to see what

40

enemy might be planning an attack on the hills that surround the valley. It can be easy to lose sight of the Shepherd in those moments.

We cannot forget that the Shepherd never leaves us in those moments in the valley. He is always with us and always watching over us. There is never a moment that we are not under the guidance and protection of the Shepherd!

We cannot live our entire lives outside of the valley. Some of the most impactful moments of our lives with the Shepherd come in those moments in the valleys. It is in those moments that we see the Shepherd fend off the enemy, providing protection for our lives and our hearts. Those are the moments when we see the Shepherd for who he really is, the one who loves and cares for us like no other!

Prayer

Lord, even when I am walking through the valley, and the path around me grows dark and overwhelming, you are there. I may not be able to see what lies ahead, causing me to have anxiety, fear, and be filled with uncertainty. The shadows can make it hard to trust, and the unknowns can feel threatening. Thank you for never leaving me to walk alone. Even when I cannot see clearly, you do. You are watching, guiding, and protecting me. No matter how dark the valley may be, you are always there. Teach me to trust you in the valley as much as I do on the mountain. Help me to trust in you, knowing that you are walking through it all with me. Amen.

Personal Reflection

• What valleys are you currently walking through?

• When life feels dark and uncertain, what fears tend to surface most strongly in your life?

• How has God shown his presence or protection in the valleys of life in the past?

• What does it look like for you to focus more on the Shepherd than the dangers that surround you in life?

Quiet Consideration

Take a deep breath and acknowledge where you may be walking through difficulty or uncertainty.

Bring those valleys honestly before the Shepherd, remembering that you are not walking through them alone.

In the stillness, reflect on the comfort found not in the absence of hardship, but in the presence of the One who walks with you.

DAY 15

When death draws near

Psalm 23:4 (KJV)
"Yea, though I walk through the valley of the shadow of death, I will fear no evil:"

Reflection

One of the more challenging valleys in life is one in which death draws near. As David describes the valley here in verse 4, he describes it as having the shadow of death. The word translated here has definitions of deep darkness, but also a place of death.

As David is reflecting on his time as a shepherd in writing this Psalm, I cannot help but wonder what type of death he experienced in the valley. Perhaps it was in the valley where he experienced the attacks of the lion and bear that he shared with Saul in 1 Samuel 17. It could be that he experienced the death of sheep in the valley.

As he writes the words of this Psalm, he references gloom and sadness, a time of sorrow and heartache. That certainly sounds like the experiences that I have had with death in life as well. In the moments before someone dies, they experience that feeling of doom and impending death. Once someone passes, there is a feeling of a shadow of death in the room. It's hard to explain, but one that I have experienced and one that David describes here in the image of the valley.

Life Application

Death is a natural part of life. Whether you have experienced the death of a close loved one or friend, at some point in life, you will. In fact, we will all have a personal experience with death at some point in our own lives that we must be prepared for.

Death is one of the most difficult valleys that we will ever walk through in life. Death can come in moments of uncertainty and tragedy. It can strike us when we least expect it. Yet, in those moments in the valley, David knew where his strength came from.

We do not have to face the aspect of death alone. Whether we are walking through the valley of the shadow of death, where someone else may have passed, or the point in time of our own lives when it is our time to pass, God will be with us. There is never a moment that he will leave us alone and expect us to make it on our own.

God has provided us a way to overcome death in this life. While death may leave us sad, we can rest assured that death in this life is not the end. In salvation, we have hope of eternal life through Jesus Christ. Death is not the end, but simply the beginning of that eternity.

Prayer

Lord, you see me in the valleys where the shadow of death falls heavy. You know the sorrows, fear, questions, and pain that can arise from the moments of loss. Death in this life can often leave us feeling helpless and uncertain. Thank you for not turning away from me in these moments and for the hope of eternal life beyond this world. When death feels close, help me remember that I am not alone. Your presence and strength will see me through. Amen.

Personal Reflection

• How has death touched your life, through loss, fear, or uncertainty?

• What emotions surface for you when thinking about death?

• In moments of grief or loss, have you sensed God's presence with you?

• How does the hope of eternal life speak to your heart?

Quiet Consideration

Take a deep breath and acknowledge where you may be walking through difficulty or uncertainty.

Bring those valleys honestly before the Shepherd, remembering that you are not walking through them alone.

In the stillness, reflect on the comfort found not in the absence of hardship, but in the presence of the One who walks with you.

DAY 16

Have no fear

Psalm 23:4 (KJV)
"Yea, though I walk through the valley of the shadow of death, I will fear no evil:"

Reflection

After reflection on some of the darkest moments of his life, David counters those thoughts with the idea of "I will fear no evil." He has just acknowledged that the valleys of life bring about fear and uncertainty. He even described the shadow of death that exists about the valley and how that can overwhelm.

David now finds strength in saying he will have no fear. No matter how dark, dismal, and dreadful the valley may be, David does not see a moment to have any fear. He remembers those moments as a shepherd with his flock. He remembers the protection and victory that he gave his own sheep in the midst of the valleys of life.

Just like his own personal experience, David continues to champion the LORD as the shepherd, knowing that God will provide victory over anything that may present in the valley. David recognized that the LORD was victorious over it all. There was nothing that might come up against the flock that could defeat the LORD. Not because of anything David had done, but because his shepherd was the LORD Jehovah!

Life Application

We live in an evil world. Simply read the news or turn on the television, and you will see nothing but evil that surrounds us each day. In many instances, we have almost become accustomed to the evil that exists in the world. It can easily cause us to fear and worry about the safety and security of our family and friends.

Just as David shared, we have no reason to fear. We have the LORD on our side. Rather than letting our lives be consumed by the fears of the things we cannot control, we should turn those fears over to the one who is in control! If you let it, the fears in the valley will consume you. Fear is one of the most powerful things in this life and is a tool that Satan loves to use against us. If you let it, it will consume your mind and heart, leaving you without the peace and comfort that the Shepherd can bring.

There is nothing that this world can bring against us that he cannot overcome. We need to put our trust in the Shepherd. No matter what the valleys in this life may bring, have no fear: the Shepherd is with you! Give those fears to the Shepherd and let him guide you to victory over them.

Prayer

Lord, you know the fears that come into my heart when my world feels dark and uncertain. The valley brings about things that can quickly overwhelm me. Fear finds a way to get into my thoughts and steals the peace you desire for me. Today, help me to trust in you. Not because the valley is easy or the danger is gone, but because you, my Shepherd, are with me. You are greater than any evil I may face, and nothing can come against you that you will not overcome. Help me to place my fears firmly in your hands. Remind me that fear does not have the final word, you do. Lead me through the valley with confidence, peace, and trust in the victory you will bring. Amen.

Personal Reflection

• What fears are most present in your life right now?

• How do these fears affect your thoughts, emotions, or decisions?

• What does it mean for you to personally say, "I will fear no evil," knowing that God is with you?

• Is there fear in your life that you need to give to God today?

Quiet Consideration

Take a deep breath and acknowledge where you may be walking through difficulty or uncertainty.

Bring those valleys honestly before the Shepherd, remembering that you are not walking through them alone.

In the stillness, reflect on the comfort found not in the absence of hardship, but in the presence of the One who walks with you.

DAY 17

Present-tense God

Psalm 23:4 (KJV)
"for thou art with me; thy rod and thy staff they comfort me."

Reflection

David continues in verse 4 after saying he has no fear by expanding on the thought. He has no fear because God is with him. David very carefully chose his words here in this moment, and it is worth exploring.

First, he did not say that God was with him. Certainly, God was with him in the days gone by. I am certain, David, just like us, recalls the times in his life when God made his presence felt, and he knew that presence from before this moment. He also did not say God will be with him, indicating a future moment of being together. David knew the role of the shepherd. A shepherd would not desert their flock. They would be with them until the end.

We see the word used here in the translation is the present tense word. David chose to use the present tense as he knew the shepherd's presence was always required. The shepherd was always present. Even though the valley might take him into places where he felt alone and in darkness, David knew that the shepherd would be with him the entire way. He would never be left alone. David was describing a present-tense God, not a past-tense or future-tense one.

Life Application

It is amazing how quickly we can forget that God is with us. We often talk about the things that God has done in the past, or the things that we hope God will do in the future. It often causes us to overlook the fact that God is present with us right now. Friends and family may accompany us so far, but then they may turn away. But God will never turn away, nor leave you!

Have you ever felt that you were alone? Perhaps you felt as though God was not present, that he did not care, or was not interested in you. The truth is the exact opposite. God is always there, he has always cared, and he is as interested in you as ever!

God is not just interested in you in the good times of life. He is also interested in you in the valleys of life. No matter what you may be going through in life, the Shepherd cares and is with you. He wants you to trust in Him and rely on Him to be your strength and guide through it all.

Prayer

Lord, thank you for being with me, not only in the memories of the past and hopes of the future, but right here and right now. At times, I may overlook your nearness. I can sometimes look back on the things you have done or toward the things I hope you will do and overlook the comfort in your presence at this moment. When I feel alone, help me remember that you are near. You are with me through every valley and every uncertainty. Help me to trust you even when I may not feel you, knowing you are still here, watching, guiding, and caring for me. Teach me to live with an awareness of your presence and draw strength from knowing that I am never alone. Amen.

Personal Reflection

• In what moments do you find yourself thinking of God more in the past or future than in the present?

• Have there been times you felt alone or unseen by God?

• What does it mean to you that God is with you right now?

• How can you intentionally acknowledge God's presence in your life throughout the day?

Quiet Consideration

Take a deep breath and acknowledge where you may be walking through difficulty or uncertainty.

Bring those valleys honestly before the Shepherd, remembering that you are not walking through them alone.

In the stillness, reflect on the comfort found not in the absence of hardship, but in the presence of the One who walks with you.

DAY 18

The rod and staff

Psalm 23:4 (KJV)
"for thou art with me; thy rod and thy staff they comfort me."

Reflection

As David continues to reflect on his time as a shepherd, he begins to consider the tools of the trade. Mentioned in the verse are the rod and staff. If you study this historically, the rod and staff refer to two different items. One is the shepherd's crook, which is rather synonymous with the lifestyle of a shepherd. It is the long stick with the hook at the end. This crook is often used to guide sheep, pulling them from danger, aligning them back with the flock, and so much more.

The other item is more of a support item. The definition indicates it is supportive of protecting the flock. It could be used to fight off wolves, lions, bears, or other predators. In other words, both items here signify correction and protection. This was not saying that David had gone astray from the shepherd. The tools had a purpose in the life of the shepherd and for the protection of the sheep.

The sheep did not always understand what the shepherd was doing when he was using the rod and staff. Sheep notoriously overlook danger, finding themselves in trouble regularly. When the shepherd would use these tools, it was a reminder to the sheep that the Shepherd knew what he was doing.

Life Application

It is often challenging for us to know exactly what God is doing in our lives as well. How many times have you ever asked the question, "Why God?" Why did this happen? Why did you let it happen? Was there a reason this needed to happen to me? These are all questions that we ask from time to time.

We might find ourselves doing exactly what we think God would have us to do, only to feel that gentle nudge of the crook moving us back into another direction. Even though we thought we were following God's will, we find the Shepherd using his tools to bring us back to the fold in a different area.

We may not always understand his purpose and plan, but we have to trust in the Shepherd's perspective. From the sheep's perspective, we cannot see and understand what is happening. From the Shepherd's perspective, he sees everything that is happening in front of us and knows exactly when to utilize his resources to pull us back into line. Though we may not understand, we must trust in the Shepherd's plan.

Prayer

Lord, thank you for watching over my life with care and intention. There are many times that I do not understand what you are doing or why you allow things to happen in my life. In those moments, I may question you and struggle to see the purpose. Help me to trust you even when I cannot see the full picture. Your perspective is higher than mine. Teach me to rest in the assurance that you know what is best, even when your guidance is uncomfortable or confusing. Amen.

Personal Reflection

• Can you recall a time God redirected your path in a way you did not expect?

• What emotions tend to surface in your life when you do not understand what God is doing?

• How does the understanding of the rod and staff as tools of protection and guidance change your views of God's correction?

• What area of your life do you need to trust to the Shepherd's perspective right now?

Quiet Consideration

Take a deep breath and acknowledge where you may be walking through difficulty or uncertainty.

Bring those valleys honestly before the Shepherd, remembering that you are not walking through them alone.

In the stillness, reflect on the comfort found not in the absence of hardship, but in the presence of the One who walks with you.

DAY 19

God of comfort

Psalm 23:4 (KJV)
"for thou art with me; thy rod and thy staff they comfort me."

Reflection

After David's reflections on the tools of the trade, he describes how these tools bring him comfort. David certainly had experience with both of these tools. If anyone was to be comforted by these two tools, it would be David, given his familiarity with the tools and the expertise in how he could operate them.

David was probably thinking back to those moments in time when he used those tools and how useful they were. He could remember times when they were used to save the life of the sheep, to save his own life, to guide the sheep, and so much more. But this was more than just the comfort that David had in these items based on their existence. It was the comfort that David experienced by their use.

David knew that when these were used in his life, they had a purpose and plan. Even though he may not have understood what they were being used for, he knew that when he felt those tools being used, it was a sign of the presence of the Shepherd. There was a purpose that the shepherd was trying to accomplish, and because the shepherd chose to use those tools for his life, it comforted him.

Life Application

We often think of God's correction as negative in our lives. Sure, God does correct us because of our sin and many failures. But God also chooses to correct us because he loves us and he wants us to have a closer walk with him.

This means that sometimes, God may need to use the tools of the trade to help us. At times, God may use his word to show us something in our lives that needs to be addressed. It may not necessarily be a sin, but it may be something that could cause an issue in our lives. We may not see it now, but God sees it and wants to address it.

Or perhaps it is the small voice that comes calling. He has spoken to you and shared something that he would like you to do. Perhaps it is a deed that he wants done. Maybe it is saying a kind word, expressing thanks to someone, or showing kindness to someone in need. Through the gentle use of the tools of the trade, the Shepherd guides us in the ways he would want us to go.

We should not take this guidance as a punishment in life. Instead, when you feel the Shepherd using the tools, take comfort. It means that God is not finished with you yet. He is still working on you and through you to accomplish his will.

Prayer

Lord, thank you for the comfort that comes from knowing you are present and actively involved in my life. I may often resist correction and feel uneasy when you begin to shape and direct my life. I may not always understand what you are doing or why you are working, but I must recognize your guidance as a sign of love. When you use your word and your voice to guide me, help me to receive it and trust you. Help me find comfort in knowing you are still working on me. Amen.

Personal Reflection

• How do you usually respond to God's correction or redirection?

• Can you recall a time when God's guidance felt uncomfortable, but later proved beneficial?

• In what ways is God guiding you right now?

• How does viewing God's correction as a sign of his presence and love change your experience of it?

Quiet Consideration

Take a deep breath and acknowledge where you may be walking through difficulty or uncertainty.

Bring those valleys honestly before the Shepherd, remembering that you are not walking through them alone.

In the stillness, reflect on the comfort found not in the absence of hardship, but in the presence of the One who walks with you.

DAY 20

God's preparation

Psalm 23:5 (KJV)
"Thou preparest a table before me in the presence of mine enemies:"

Reflection

As we enter verse 5 of Psalm 23, the tone takes a different turn. David seems to be transitioning from a time of reflection about his time as a shepherd and relating it to God to identifying a difference in how God acts as his shepherd. He starts verse 5 by discussing a table that is being prepared.

As you continue to study the original text, the idea of preparation has the meaning of being set out, put into order, and specifically placed. As you move into the concept of the table, it is the idea of a table being prepared for a meal. A meal in which everything was prepared carefully for those who were going to eat.

As David's transition now focuses on the table, he recognizes the preparation for his life that God has made. Nothing about his life was set in place by accident. God had a specific purpose and plan for it all. Just as someone who might set out a table to prepare for a meal and set things in a specific place, God had ordained things in his life out of divine preparation. God knew what David would face and how he needed to be prepared to address it.

Life Application

God's divine preparation is not always easy to see. There are many times in life that we see the problem arise long before we understand the preparation was made. I can think of several examples from my own life. Perhaps a bill came due long before I realized that God was already at work providing the source for the money to pay that bill. If you look back on your life, you can no doubt share similar preparation by God for things in your life.

Each thing that comes into our lives has appeared with a purpose and a plan. No matter the difficulty or circumstance, God knows exactly what he is doing. He knows what we have need of and when we will need it. We may experience the problem, but God has already been at work on the solution!

We have to trust that God's preparation is always in the perfect time and place. It would be easy to go into a problem if we always knew the solution. How would we ever learn to trust the Shepherd if we always saw the solution ahead of time? Instead, God chooses to make the preparation and reveal it to us in due time. This forces us to continue to rely on and trust in him as our shepherd.

Prayer

Lord, thank you for being God who prepares for me long before I ever see the need. I may often focus on the problem in front of me and struggle to see that you are already at work in the circumstance behind the scenes. When answers are delayed and solutions are unclear, I can sometimes become anxious and impatient. Help me to trust in your preparation and timing, even when I cannot see it. Remind me that nothing in my life is by accident. You are in control and handle everything in due time. Teach me to rest in you and rely on you as my Shepherd. Amen.

Personal Reflection

• Do you recall a time when God had already prepared a solution before you fully recognized the problem?

• What situation in your life now requires trusting in God's preparation?

• How does viewing your life as intentionally prepared by God change how you see challenges?

• Is God inviting you to learn through trusting his timing right now?

Quiet Consideration

Pause and consider how intentionally God has prepared and provided for your life.

Reflect on the invitation to sit at His table, cared for and sustained even in the presence of opposition.

As you sit quietly, allow gratitude to shape your thoughts, recognizing the abundance that flows from His grace.

DAY 21

Eating at God's table

Psalm 23:5 (KJV)
"Thou preparest a table before me in the presence of mine enemies:"

Reflection

As we continue to examine verse 5, David explains that a table was prepared before him. As we already discussed, this was a specifically planned table. Each person and item had a specific place. What is perhaps the most fascinating thing to see here is not necessarily found in the meal, but specifically with the table.

This was not just any regular table that was before David. If you study the original text, the word translated as "table" is that of the King's private table. David recognized that this was not the type of table that he had experienced as a shepherd out in the fields. This was a special table.

This table was one that required a special invitation. Not everyone was able to sit at the king's private table. This table was reserved for family, close friends, and honored guests. I have often wondered if this was on David's mind when he invited Mephibosheth to sit at the King's table in 2 Samuel 9. This special invitation was an honor for Mephibosheth. David gives a comparison to that same experience here in Psalm 23, where he says he was invited to a table spread before him.

Life Application

God's table is an amazing image to think about, especially given our status as children of God. Not one of us is worthy to sit at the King's table. We are far from royalty and deserving of such treatment. But as Paul shares in the New Testament, we are adopted into the family of

God. This is not because of our own actions, but because of the sacrifice of Jesus Christ on the cross.

This not only gives us access to the King's table but also access to a feast beyond measure. The table is not a picture of a simple meal, but rather an extravagant preparation made for a feast. It was intended that no one would leave this table hungry.

In our Christian lives, God has prepared a table before us to enjoy spiritually. We are given this privilege through Jesus Christ. This table has been prepared specifically for us so that we might sit down in a safe and secure environment and be completely filled. It is the idea of a royal banquet that is filled with enough provisions to fill you to complete satisfaction. There is nothing in this world that can provide that level of satisfaction in our lives. It can only be found at God's table!

Prayer

Lord, I am humbled by the invitation you have given me to sit and eat at your table. Not as a stranger, but as one welcomed as part of the family. The world would have me believe I do not deserve to be at this table, given all my faults and failures. But you remind me that this invitation is not because of what I have done, but because of what Christ has done for me. You purposefully prepared a place for me to receive what you have provided so that I might find full satisfaction. Teach me to continue to identify as your child and find true satisfaction in your presence. Amen.

Personal Reflection

• How do you feel about the idea of being invited to the King's table?

• What thoughts and feelings make it difficult for you to accept the invitation of God to his table?

• In what ways have you looked to the world to satisfy your needs that only God can meet?

• How can you make better use of your time at God's table?

Quiet Consideration

Pause and consider how intentionally God has prepared and provided for your life.

Reflect on the invitation to sit at His table, cared for and sustained even in the presence of opposition.

As you sit quietly, allow gratitude to shape your thoughts, recognizing the abundance that flows from His grace.

DAY 22

In front of the enemy

Psalm 23:5 (KJV)
"Thou preparest a table before me in the presence of mine enemies."

Reflection

As David thinks about the moments of sitting down at the King's table, he shares an interesting perspective. Typically, the King's table was a safe space for the king and those who dined with the King. Rather than talking about the safety of the King's table, David mentions that the table was prepared before him in the presence of his enemies.

As David considered his place, sitting at the King's table and eating of the King's food, he did not deserve to be there. He also realized that there were many who attempted to keep him from reaching this position as well. Throughout David's life, many had tried to keep him from reaching the potential that God had for him. In spite of all their efforts, here was David sitting at the King's table.

Satan could try all that he wanted, but he could not prevent David from being at the King's table. He could put all of his efforts into trying to prevent David from being supplied with nourishment at the King's table, but nothing could stop it. David could sit down with full confidence that nothing would be able to stop his dining at the King's table and for him to be fulfilled.

Life Application

There are many things in this life that will try to come between us and our relationship with God. Satan would love nothing more than to keep you from being filled with spiritual nourishment at the King's table. Yet, even in the presence of the enemy, God still spreads out the feast and prepares for you to be filled.

David could have easily allowed these people to keep him from reaching the King's table. Instead, he followed God and trusted in God. That same table is spread out before any child of God, but we often allow others to prevent us from enjoying it. Have you ever heard someone say you are not good enough for God to care for you? Maybe they have even shared the question of how God could love someone like you, given all that you have done in this life.

David certainly knew these types of questions in his life. He had done a lot of things that could be used against him by others, including Satan. Yet, he did not let that stand in his way, and neither should we. Because we are God's children, we are on the winning side. We can claim victory and enjoy the King's table, no matter what the enemy might say.

Prayer

Lord, thank you for inviting me to your table in the presence of my enemies. It can be easy to be intimidated, feel unworthy, or be distracted by those who oppose me. Their voices can overwhelm or even rise up in my heart as a distraction, preventing me from enjoying fulfillment at your table. Thank you for reminding me that your table is secure. No accusation, failure, or opposition can remove me from what you have prepared for me. Help me to stop listening to those who say I do not belong and to fully trust that you are greater than any enemy I may face. Amen.

Personal Reflection

• What voices, internal or external, have tried to tell you that you do not belong at God's table?

• How have you let opposition or criticism prevent you from enjoying God's table?

• What does it look like for you to sit comfortably at the King's table today, trusting that your place in Christ is secure?

Quiet Consideration

Pause and consider how intentionally God has prepared and provided for your life.

Reflect on the invitation to sit at His table, cared for and sustained even in the presence of opposition.

As you sit quietly, allow gratitude to shape your thoughts, recognizing the abundance that flows from His grace.

DAY 23

When God anoints you

Psalm 23:5 (KJV)
"Thou anointest my head with oil; my cup runneth over."

Reflection

In David's day, a common practice was to pour oil over the head of distinguished guests as part of special feasts. A similar event took place in the New Testament when Mary used the oil with Jesus. David was no stranger to being anointed. He had been anointed King by Samuel. As the King, he could have potentially experienced the anointing of guests as part of this ritual as well.

David knew the honor and responsibility that came with being anointed. It was a special honor, but not one to be taken lightly. The anointing came with responsibility in the case of David. Once anointed as King, he had to live a different life from the one he had as a shepherd.

For a distinguished guest being anointed, it was a moment of recognition that drew attention to them. Everyone knew that the guest was present and the special honor that was bestowed on them.

Life Application

While we may have never been anointed as the King of Israel, like David, we have all received an amazing gift. We have been anointed as Children of God. This marks a significant change in who we are and whose we are.

When we accept Christ as Savior, our lives reflect a new allegiance. At that moment, we declare that we are no longer living for ourselves but are living our lives dedicated to God. We no longer serve our purpose, but God's purpose. We no longer strive for our own things, but for the things of God.

But do we live that example to others? Do they see us as truly having the anointing of God on our lives? Being anointed by God is a unique recognition. It aligns perfectly with the concepts of being asked to sit at the King's table. But with that anointing comes responsibility.

As adopted members of God's family, we must realize that we now represent the family everywhere we go and in everything we do. That is a tremendous responsibility. One that has been given special recognition by God.

Prayer

Lord, thank you for the anointing you have placed on my life as a Child of God. This is not because of my worthiness, but because of your love. You have marked me as your own and welcomed me into your family through Jesus Christ. Help me to live from that identity. Help me not forget my responsibility as your child, being an example of your love to others. Teach me to represent you through a life shaped by humility, obedience, and love. May my life reflect the honor and grace you have given me. Amen.

Personal Reflection

• What does it mean for you to be personally anointed as a Child of God?

• In what ways do you sometimes feel pressure to "live up" to your faith rather than live by grace through faith?

• How might your daily choices and interactions reflect your belonging to Christ's family?

• What does it look like for you to walk confidently as a Child of God without fear?

Quiet Consideration

Pause and consider how intentionally God has prepared and provided for your life.

Reflect on the invitation to sit at His table, cared for and sustained even in the presence of opposition.

As you sit quietly, allow gratitude to shape your thoughts, recognizing the abundance that flows from His grace.

DAY 24

Is your cup full?

Psalm 23:5 (KJV)
"Thou anointest my head with oil; my cup runneth over."

Reflection

Just after describing how he was anointed with oil as the distinguished guest, David continues by saying his cup runneth over. David is not simply talking about a cup that has been filled up. The idea that David is sharing here is that his cup has been filled and is overflowing.

This aligns with the idea of the feast, where there was plenty to offer. This would be an image of someone who was given a cup, and even though the cup was full, they continued to fill the cup so that there was an overabundance of liquid.

David was not a stranger to having a full cup. Otherwise, he would have conveniently left this out of the Psalm. Instead, David is describing the fullness that comes from spending time at God's table. Not only does he prepare a feast that can completely satisfy, but it will also cause your cup to run over!

One writer I read described it as a cup sitting on a saucer. Once the cup becomes so full, the liquid inside the cup begins to spill out and over the side into the saucer. In other words, the cup is so full that it begins to have an impact on others around it.

Life Application

It could be easy for us to say that it is someone else's responsibility to impact others around us. Yet, we are the ones who have been invited as distinguished guests to the king's table. We have been anointed as children of God through Jesus Christ. So, as we sit at the table, our desire should be that our cup becomes so full that it begins to run over.

When our cup runs over, it can have a tremendous impact on those around us. When our hearts become so full of the love of God, the love of God flows out and is easily displayed for those around us. When our spirit is overjoyed in the things of God, it becomes easy for us to share about God and his goodness with others around us.

God does not overfill our cups so that we might save what was given for a later time. Our cups are overfilled so that it spills out onto others, so that they might experience a little taste of what we are experiencing as well. We should not be afraid for our cup to be full. We should be afraid if our cup is not so full that others may experience it.

Prayer

Lord, thank you for the abundance you have given me in my life. You have given me not just enough, but more than enough. You give fully and freely! You have invited me to your table, satisfied my soul, and continued to pour out until my cup has overflowed. Help me receive what you have given without any hesitation. When my cup is full, help me to let it spill out naturally to those around me so that they might experience you in a greater way. May my life reflect the abundance I have found in your presence, overflowing in a way that points others to you. Amen.

Personal Reflection

• In what ways have you experienced God's abundance in your life?

• What keeps you from believing that God wants to fill your cup completely?

• How have you seen the overflow of God's work in your life impact others around you?

• What does it look like for you to live a life with overflow rather than reservation in this season?

Quiet Consideration

Pause and consider how intentionally God has prepared and provided for your life.

Reflect on the invitation to sit at His table, cared for and sustained even in the presence of opposition.

As you sit quietly, allow gratitude to shape your thoughts, recognizing the abundance that flows from His grace.

DAY 25

Unending goodness and mercy

Psalm 23:6 (KJV)
"Surely goodness and mercy shall follow me all the days of my life:"

Reflection

David is now reflecting on the benefits of God. He has been thinking about the feast that God has prepared at the King's table. He shared how his cup overflowed out of abundance. Now, David mentions the goodness and mercy of God.

David was no stranger to the mercy of God. As I have already mentioned, David was far from a perfect person. He had made many mistakes. He had committed adultery, planned a murder, disobeyed God, and much more. If David were alive in our day today, he would have been asked to step down as King.

Even with all his faults and failures, David still experienced the love of God and knew about the goodness and mercy of God. God could have been finished with David. He could have said, "David, you have made too many mistakes. I need to find someone new."

Instead, God provided forgiveness, mercy, and goodness. David certainly faced punishment for his sin. He knew what God's judgment looked like on his life. But even amid that judgment, David knew that God was good to him and had shown him tremendous mercy.

Life Application

There are tremendous benefits in being a child of God. We have an anointing on our life, fulfillment at the King's table and an abundance that will cause our cup to overflow. We can also each share about our experience with the goodness and mercy of God.

Mercy is the kindness of God in withholding what we truly deserve. If we are all honest, for all of our sins and shortcomings, not one of us deserves the mercy and goodness of God. Yet, God gives it to us as one of the unmerited benefits of being a child of God. That is not saying we have a free pass to do whatever we want. There are still judgments for our sins.

It does mean that God loves us so much that he has given us mercy and goodness that we did not deserve. We have experienced forgiveness that we did not deserve. We have been given protection that we did not deserve. We were given sustenance that we did not deserve. All because of the goodness and mercy of Almighty God!

Prayer

Lord, thank you for your goodness that I have not earned and your mercy that I do not deserve. In my life, I see moments of failure, weakness, and disobedience. Yet, you have not turned away from me. You still love me. Thank you for your mercy that withholds what I deserve and your goodness that gives me what I could never earn. Even when I fail you, you continue to love me and lead me. Help me to live with a heart of gratitude for the love and mercy you have shown in my life. Amen.

Personal Reflection

• Where have you experienced the goodness of God in your life?

• How have you personally experienced the mercy of God, withholding what you deserved?

• Do you ever struggle to believe that God can still be good to you after mistakes?

• How does living with daily awareness of God's goodness and mercy change your attitude, humility, or gratitude?

Quiet Consideration

Slow down and reflect on the story your life is telling.

Consider how God's goodness and mercy have followed you through every season, shaping who you are becoming.

In this quiet moment, allow your heart to rest in the hope of dwelling with the Shepherd—not only now, but forever.

DAY 26

It lasts forever

Psalm 23:6 (KJV)
"Surely goodness and mercy shall follow me all the days of my life:"

Reflection

As David continues to think about the benefits of God, he considers that not only has he experienced the goodness and mercy of God right now, but he also acknowledges that these benefits last forever. David was experienced enough in life to realize that not many things last forever. He had seen a king's reign come to an end in his life. He had seen other lives come to an end.

He knew and understood that his time here on this earth was numbered. Not one of us will live here in this world forever. Yet, the benefits that have been bestowed on our lives do not go away. They will follow us all the days of our lives!

In this moment, David is saying that in the good times and the bad times, God's goodness and mercy will follow me. Up on the mountains and in those valleys that I was writing about a few moments ago, God's goodness and mercy will follow me. It was a reassurance to David that no matter where his life may take him, God would never abandon him. He would always be there, with goodness and mercy to bestow. If David's cup was not already overflowing, it certainly should be by now given this thought!

Life Application

We do not know where our lives may go. For some, life takes unexpected turns as the loss of a loved one changes all of our plans. For others, career challenges and changes may force us out of what we had planned.

76

There are so many different scenarios to consider that it would be challenging to include all of them here.

There is a good chance you have already experienced events in your life that have led you to change your plans. We do not always know where our lives may go, but God does. He knows exactly what will come into our lives and how it will impact us.

No matter what may come into our lives, God's goodness and mercy will follow us all the way through. It will not go part of the way and stop. It will not follow us until the path becomes too difficult to continue on and leave us stranded. It will continue with us all the way through, right until our last moments on this earth. What an encouraging and refreshing thought that we can take courage in!

Prayer

Lord, thank you for the assurance that your goodness and mercy do not come and go in the seasons of life. There are times that I might worry about what lies ahead and how future changes may impact me. But I can rest assured that in those unsettling times, you will remain faithful and true. No matter where my path may lead, you will not abandon me. Your goodness and mercy will follow me wherever I may go. Help me to trust you with the future that I cannot see. Give me peace in knowing that whatever may come, I will never walk alone. Amen.

Personal Reflection

• What uncertainties about the future concern you the most?

• Where can you see God's goodness and mercy following you in your life to this point?

• Does knowing that God's goodness and mercy follow you throughout all the days of your life bring you comfort?

• How can you more fully trust God with the unknowns of your life?

Quiet Consideration

Slow down and reflect on the story your life is telling.

Consider how God's goodness and mercy have followed you through every season, shaping who you are becoming.

In this quiet moment, allow your heart to rest in the hope of dwelling with the Shepherd—not only now, but forever.

DAY 27

A life's story

Psalm 23:6 (KJV)
"Surely goodness and mercy shall follow me all the days of my life:"

Reflection

As we read through this Psalm, we are reading about someone who is reflecting on life. David has spent a lot of time reflecting on his time as a shepherd. He compared those moments in his life to the relationship that he has with God as his shepherd.

Now, it is almost as if David is looking back over his life as a whole. Perhaps he is in an extremely reflective state, and he mentions all the days of his life. David certainly was thankful for the goodness and mercy that provided encouragement as he faced the uncertain future. But what about the story of his life?

David knew that he was writing a story with the life that he lived each and every day. That story was leaving a legacy. His legacy was filled with ups and downs, as I have already shared. David knew that the future would share his mistakes. But now, as he reflected on his life, he knew that he had an opportunity to do something special with what remained in his life. He was not the young shepherd that he once was, but he was not in the final moments of his life either. This was a unique opportunity for David.

Life Application

Not one of us knows when our last moments on this earth will be, yet we are all writing the story of our lives. I often think back about friends and loved ones who have passed on from this life and remember details about their lives. I remember the stories that they shared and the memories that we all made. Their lives left a story about who they were and the God that they believed in.

What will our life's story tell about us? Will our story be one of faith and dedication to God, our Shepherd? Will others be able to see that we lived our lives for God, serving him rather than serving our own desires and our own interests?

Our lives were not given to us simply to live for ourselves. They were given to us so that we might live them for God. Every moment of every day should be lived writing the story about how we love God and want to serve him.

Our hope should be that our story points others to God. We should want to live our lives so that anyone who meets us knows we serve God and live our lives for Him.

Prayer

Lord, thank you for the life that you have given to me and the story that you are allowing me to write with my life every day. I do not always live with the awareness of the legacy that my choices are creating. It is easy to move through life focused on the moment rather than the larger story. Help me to live intentionally, with gratitude and humility for what lies ahead. May the story of my life reflect you to a world who needs you. Use the days I have left to point others to you. Amen.

Personal Reflection

• If you think about your life's story right now, what themes do you see?

• What do you hope others will remember about your life and relationship with God?

• Are there areas of your life where you sense God inviting you to write a different chapter moving forward?

• How can you live your life today in a way that honors God and aligns with the story you hope your life will tell?

Quiet Consideration

Slow down and reflect on the story your life is telling.

Consider how God's goodness and mercy have followed you through every season, shaping who you are becoming.

In this quiet moment, allow your heart to rest in the hope of dwelling with the Shepherd—not only now, but forever.

DAY 28

Life with God

Psalm 23:6 (KJV)
"and I will dwell in the house of the LORD for ever."

Reflection

David moves on from this moment of reflection and the thought about life to a moment where he shares what he hopes happens in his future. There are several things that can be seen in this verse, but I want to examine the statement about dwelling first.

When David talks about dwelling, this is the idea of settling in, abiding, and remaining. David recognizes that God's goodness and mercy will follow him throughout his life, but he acknowledges that there is a risk he could depart from a close relationship with God.

David is not realizing this because he has things on his mind that he plans to do. He is not sharing his intention to commit some heinous crime or sin. David is talking from a place of maturity in life.

He recognizes that the enemies he spoke of just a few moments ago will continue to rise against him. They will continue to pressure him and challenge his walk with God. He may not purposefully seek to depart from walking with the Shepherd, but it could happen if he does not commit his heart to remaining, settling in, and abiding in God.

Life Application

We each understand that our lives are a story that we are writing, yet none of us knows the future of what our story might hold. We can be certain of one thing, however. No matter where our future will take us, Satan wants nothing more than for us to depart from a close walk with

God. He does not want us to have that close relationship with the Shepherd that David described in the earlier verses.

Each of us must commit in our hearts that we want to dwell with God. This is not a "hope" or a "wish" but rather something that we are setting as a top priority in our lives. It is the idea of saying that no matter what may come against me in life, I want to make sure that I am walking with God through it all.

That is certainly easier said than done. What David knows, however, is that if this is not a priority in his heart, he will never follow through. The first time something comes into his life, he will depart from God and go in a different direction.

We must commit our lives to dwelling with God. We know that Satan will not stop with the attacks on our lives. He will bring things and attempt to draw us away from God. Dwelling with God has to be a priority, or it will easily fall by the wayside.

Prayer

Lord, thank you for the goodness and mercy that will follow me every day of my life. Even with all that you have done, I realize that it is possible for me to drift away from you if I am not intentional in remaining close to you. Pressures, distractions, and challenges in life can slowly pull my attention away. Today, help me to settle my heart in you. Strengthen my resolve to walk with you in every moment. Teach me what it means to truly dwell with you. Amen.

Personal Reflection

• What does dwelling with God mean to you personally?

• What tends to draw your heart away from closeness with God?

• Have you seen the effects of drifting versus abiding in your life?

• How can you be intentional in taking steps to make dwelling with God a priority in your life?

Quiet Consideration

Slow down and reflect on the story your life is telling.

Consider how God's goodness and mercy have followed you through every season, shaping who you are becoming.

In this quiet moment, allow your heart to rest in the hope of dwelling with the Shepherd—not only now, but forever.

DAY 29

The house of the LORD

Psalm 23:6 (KJV)
"and I will dwell in the house of the LORD for ever."

Reflection

Throughout David's life, he had an affection for the house of the LORD. In many Psalms, he spoke about the house of the LORD. It was even in his heart to build the temple, but we find that God took that away from David due to David being a man of war. Even with that being taken away, David still helped in the preparation for the temple.

As David thinks about the house of the LORD, he recognizes that this is where God abides. As David understands the importance of dwelling with God, he also recognizes the importance of God's house as part of that dwelling.

David did not mean that he wanted to actually live in the tabernacle or temple. David wanted his life to be one as though he was regularly known in the presence of God. This was not accomplished by simply stating he was a follower of God, but was an action lived out by faithfully attending worship and spending time with God on a personal level. David was certainly known throughout his writings and the story of his life for his conversations with God.

Life Application

In our day, many people lack the affection for God like David. They do not appreciate the house of the LORD or spending time with him on a personal level. These are two of the most important things that we can do as Christians, however!

God did not design our lives for solitude. His design for our lives included the idea of collective worship. Even with the development of new technology that makes collective worship easier than ever, many people still ignore the important role that the house of the LORD plays in their lives.

Just as important are the personal conversations we have in prayer with God. In the Garden of Eden, God desired to have personal communication with us. Even though sin entered the world and caused separation, this does not change God's desire to talk with us. He still wants to hear from his children.

For many Christians, the house of the LORD has become a strained relationship. Prayer can often become an overlooked resource. At times, it is completely forgotten. Our desire should be that everyone around us knows that we are people of prayer and with an affection for the house of the LORD.

Prayer

Lord, thank you for inviting me into your presence. This invitation is not just for a few moments, but for a life marked by closeness with you. I am grateful that you desire to dwell with me and welcome me into places where your presence is known and felt. Help my affection for you not to be distracted or strained. Renew my love for your presence in private conversation and collective worship. May my life reflect a deep affection for you, not just in words, but in how I live each day. Amen.

Personal Reflection

• What role has the house of the LORD played in your life?

• How would you describe your current prayer life?

• What pulls your attention away from time with God, personally and in worship?

• What does a deeper affection for God's presence look like in your life?

Quiet Consideration

Slow down and reflect on the story your life is telling.

Consider how God's goodness and mercy have followed you through every season, shaping who you are becoming.

In this quiet moment, allow your heart to rest in the hope of dwelling with the Shepherd—not only now, but forever.

DAY 30

Being ready for forever

Psalm 23:6 (KJV)
"and I will dwell in the house of the LORD for ever."

Reflection

David's final thoughts in Psalm 23 revolve around dwelling with God. He ends it with the idea of dwelling in the house of the LORD forever. As I have already mentioned, David knew that his days on this earth were numbered. He had experienced death in many ways by this point in life. He knew that not only were his days numbered, but that there was more to this life than simply what he was living now.

He has already reflected on his past, he has considered his present anointed position with God, and now he thinks about his future with God forever. It is the completion of David's full life story. He knew that once his days on earth were finished, he had forever ahead of him.

As David reflects on this moment, it seems that he is saying that to prepare for the future, he is committing every moment of his life to the LORD. It is as if David is saying, for everything you have done, for everything that you continue to do, and for the future of forever, I will give my entire life to you. There are a lot of people who are not prepared for their moments of forever, but that does not seem to be the case for David. He appears to be ready forever.

Life Application

Forever can come into our lives at any point in time. Scripture tells us that our lives are but a vapor and that we do not know when our time will be over. Most of us have experienced a moment when we have lost others in life earlier than we would have anticipated. The truth is, forever could be here for us before we know it. What is even worse is if forever arrives before we are ready for it.

There are two aspects of being ready for forever that each person in life must address. The first is being ready and having accepted Jesus Christ as Savior. This is the only way to be ready for eternity in the presence of God in Heaven. The Bible clearly says that there is no other way to enter into Heaven, except by the forgiveness that is found in the blood of Jesus Christ.

The second preparation that must be made is that we live our lives knowing that forever could arrive at any moment. Our lives should be lived with no regrets, understanding that we may find ourselves in the presence of God at any time. As David, we should commit our lives to God in every moment that we have left. The longer we wait, the closer forever becomes, and the valuable moments we miss being able to live for God.

Prayer

Lord, thank you for the hope of forever that you have placed before me. I am grateful that this life is not the end and that you have prepared an eternal dwelling for those who belong to you. In the days that I have remaining, I want to place my trust fully in you. Thank you for the gift of salvation in Jesus Christ. Teach me to surrender my present and my future into your hands. May my life reflect a readiness for eternity, shaped by love and devotion for you and your will. Help me walk with you until the day I dwell with you forever. Amen.

Personal Reflection

• What comes to mind when you think about forever?

• How confident are you in your readiness for eternity through Jesus?

• In what ways does remembering that life is temporary shape how you want to live today?

• Are you committing every remaining moment of your life to God?

Quiet Consideration

Slow down and reflect on the story your life is telling.

Consider how God's goodness and mercy have followed you through every season, shaping who you are becoming.

In this quiet moment, allow your heart to rest in the hope of dwelling with the Shepherd—not only now, but forever.

About the Author

Jared Dyson is a writer and ministry leader passionate about helping others encounter God through Scripture, reflection, and prayer. His heart for ministry is rooted in a desire to point people back to the life-giving truth of God's Word and to encourage a deeper, daily walk with the Shepherd who restores, leads, and sustains.

Jared's writing flows from personal study, lived faith, and a commitment to creating space for others to slow down and reflect on who God is and how He is at work in their lives. Through Another Well Ministries, he seeks to help people draw from the wells God has provided, finding renewal, hope, and spiritual strength for every season of life.

Jared holds a degree from Liberty University and continues to serve in ministry, trusting God to use both the quiet moments of reflection and the everyday experiences of life to shape hearts and draw people closer to Him.

To learn more or access additional resources, visit: www.anotherwell.org